A-Z

_of_

AUSTRALIAN ANIMALS

ALSO BY JENNIFER COSSINS

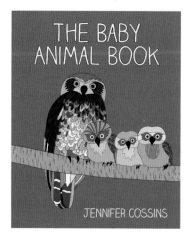

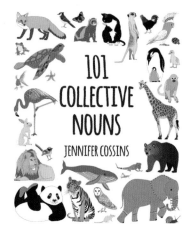

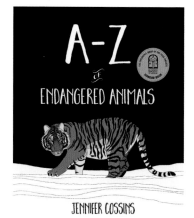

A-Z

OF

AUSTRALIAN ANIMALS

JENNIFER COSSINS

LOTHIAN
Children's Books

A Lothian Children's Book

Published in Australia and New Zealand in 2018
by Hachette Australia
Level 17, 207 Kent Street, Sydney NSW 2000
www.hachettechildrens.com.au

1 3 5 7 9 10 8 6 4 2

 A catalogue record for this
book is available from the
National Library of Australia

ISBN 978 0 7344 1858 6 (hardback)

Cover design by Seymour Designs
Text design by Red Parka Press
Typesetting by Seymour Designs
Colour reproduction by Splitting Image
Printed in China by Toppan Leefung Printing Limited

THIS BOOK IS FOR MY DAD, PHILIP COSSINS,
WHO IS DOING IT TOUGH BUT NEVER STOPS BELIEVING.

I'M SO PROUD TO BE YOUR DAUGHTER.

CONTENTS

INTRODUCTION

Australia is home to an amazing range of unique and unusual animals. As one of the world's largest countries by land mass, we have a wide variety of ecosystems: deserts, tropical forests, coastline, reefs, swamps, forests and mountains. Having so many types of habitat has allowed a huge diversity of plant and animal life to evolve.

Australia (along with New Guinea) has been isolated from much of the rest of the world since it split from the supercontinent Gondwana and began to drift north about 45 million years ago. At this time, the global climate was cooling and the world suffered from a loss of animal diversity. But in Australia, the drift north meant that our climate stayed about the same and our diversity was maintained. In addition, the isolation created an environment in which our animals evolved without impact from other continents.

In this book, you will meet 26 of Australia's amazing animals – one for each letter of the alphabet. All these animals are native to Australia, meaning they occur here naturally. Most are also endemic, meaning they don't occur anywhere else in the world. In fact, we have a higher proportion of endemic animals than just about anywhere else on earth!

Australia is especially well known for marsupials. A marsupial is a mammal that raises its young in a pouch. Some famous marsupials you will find in this book are kangaroos, koalas and wallabies. But you will also find some lesser known marsupials, including bilbies, pygmy possums and numbats.

Probably the most unusual of our native animals are the echidna and the platypus. They are the only egg-laying mammals in the world and you can learn more about them later in this book.

Not to be outdone by the furry mammals, Australia's feathered fauna is also beautiful and varied. We have more than 800 bird species, ranging from the tiny zebra finch to the large flightless cassowary, and more than half of these are not found anywhere else in the world. Particularly colourful are the 56 species of parrot that call Australia home, including the yellow-tailed black cockatoo, the mulga parrot and the galah.

A somewhat contentious inclusion in this book is the dingo, Australia's infamous wild dog. Dingoes are believed to have arrived in Australia from Asia around 4000 years ago. Thought to be descended from the South Asian grey wolf, dingoes adapted well to Australian conditions and became an integral part of our ecosystem. While some dispute their standing as a native species, they clearly differ from invaders such as rabbits and foxes, which arrived with European settlers and have wreaked havoc on Australia's native wildlife. I feel the dingo deserves its place in this book.

Creating an A to Z list requires difficult decisions. How, for instance, to choose between the koala and the kookaburra? Or the echidna and the emu? And of course, there is the thorny issue of the letter X. Seeing as there is no Australian animal whose common name begins with X, I looked to the scientific names and was pleased to find the beautiful Macleay's honeyeater. Honeyeaters are a large and diverse part of Australia's birdlife, with more than 187 different species known to be native to Australia and New Guinea. They are also much loved in Australian society and I think an important addition to any book about our wildlife.

So it's time to turn the page and begin your journey through the alphabet and discover for yourself some of Australia's most beautiful, interesting and iconic animals. Enjoy!

A IS FOR...

SCIENTIFIC NAME: ALCEDO AZUREA	SIZE: 17-19 CENTIMETRES TALL

The azure kingfisher is one of Australia's smallest and most beautiful kingfishers and is named for the dazzling blues and purples of their head and back feathers. They are found in most parts of northern and eastern Australia, as well as a few islands in Indonesia and New Guinea.

Azure kingfishers form monogamous pairs that will fiercely defend their territory. They like to be near water and can often be seen perched on branches over freshwater creeks or lakes.

Azure kingfishers plunge from overhead branches into the water to catch their prey, usually fish, insects, crustaceans or even small frogs. The kingfisher's prey is often then bashed against a branch before being swallowed whole.

INTERESTING FACT: AZURE KINGFISHERS BUILD NESTS IN BURROWS IN RIVER OR LAKE BANKS, MAKING THEM ESPECIALLY SUSCEPTIBLE TO FLOODING.

AZURE KINGFISHER

B IS FOR . . .

SCIENTIFIC NAME: MACROTIS LAGOTIS	SIZE: 29–55 CENTIMETRES LONG

Bilbies are ground-dwelling marsupials that are part of the bandicoot family. Unlike other types of bandicoot, bilbies have large, rabbit-like ears.

Bilbies like to burrow and one bilby may make up to 12 different burrows within its territory. They are nocturnal animals that forage at night for seeds, fruit, insects and fungi.

There once were two species of bilby in Australia: the lesser bilby and the greater bilby. Both habitat loss and competition from introduced species have led to the extinction of the lesser bilby. The greater bilby survives but is endangered due to the same threats and their numbers continue to fall.

INTERESTING FACT: THE BILBY'S ICONIC BIG EARS HAVE MADE IT A POPULAR AUSTRALIAN ALTERNATIVE TO THE EASTER BUNNY.

BILBY

C IS FOR ...

SCIENTIFIC NAME: CASUARIUS CASUARIUS	SIZE: 1.5-2 METRES TALL

Cassowaries are large and distinctive flightless birds. The cassowary is Australia's heaviest bird and the females are bigger and more aggressive than the males.

Their habitat is the rainforests of north-east Queensland but they can also be found in southern parts of New Guinea. Cassowaries eat fruit and are responsible for much of the distribution of seeds in the rainforest.

Cassowaries are not monogamous. Females may lay eggs in the nests of several different males each season. It is then the males' job to incubate the eggs and raise the chicks.

INTERESTING FACT: CASSOWARIES HAVE A DAGGER-LIKE MIDDLE TOE THAT CAN GROW TO AROUND 12-13 CENTIMETRES.

CASSOWARY

D IS FOR...

SCIENTIFIC NAME: CANIS DINGO	SIZE: 1.2-1.5 METRES LONG

Dingoes are Australia's wild dogs. They are thought to have descended from the South Asian grey wolf and were introduced to Australia by Asian seafarers more than 4000 years ago, long before European settlement.

While some dispute its status as a native animal, Australia has certainly adopted the dingo as its own and it has become a cultural icon. Dingo images can be seen in Aboriginal rock carvings and cave paintings and they feature prominently in stories from the Dreaming.

Dingoes are carnivores that both hunt and scavenge. They are usually solitary hunters but sometimes form packs to hunt larger prey, such as kangaroos. In a dingo pack, only the dominant dingoes breed, while the others help look after the pups.

INTERESTING FACT: UNLIKE DOMESTIC DOGS, DINGOES RARELY BARK, BUT COMMUNICATE MORE OFTEN WITH VARIOUS TYPES OF HOWLS AND GROWLS.

DINGO

E IS FOR . . .

SCIENTIFIC NAME: TACHYGLOSSUS ACULEATUS	SIZE: 30–45 CENTIMETRES LONG

Echidnas are common across all parts of Australia but are rarely seen as they are very shy creatures.

Alongside platypuses, echidnas are the world's only living monotremes, which means they are the only mammals that lay eggs. Echidnas have tiny mouths that can open about 5 millimetres, but they have long tongues, up to 18 centimetres, which dart out to catch ants and termites with sticky saliva.

Although they are normally solitary creatures, long lines of echidnas can be seen during the annual breeding season. The female echidna leads the group and is followed by up to ten males. Eventually she will decide to mate with the most persistent male, and two weeks later will lay a single egg. The egg stays in her pouch for ten days until it hatches. The baby then remains in the pouch until its spines begin to grow at about three months old.

INTERESTING FACT: A BABY ECHIDNA IS CALLED A PUGGLE.

ECHIDNA

F IS FOR . . .

| SCIENTIFIC NAME: CHLAMYDOSAURUS KINGII | SIZE: 45-90 CENTIMETRES LONG |

Frillneck lizards are found in the tropical regions of northern Australia as well as parts of southern New Guinea. They get their name from the large frill around their necks, which is usually folded loosely but extends out wide to become a formidable sight when the lizard feels threatened.

Frillneck lizards spend most of their time in trees, due to the excellent camouflage they provide. Frillnecks eat mostly insects and other invertebrates, but also the occasional small reptile.

The gender of frillneck lizards is determined by the temperature of the nest, with a hotter nest producing more females. Frillneck lizard hatchlings emerge from the egg fully formed, frills and all, and fend for themselves from birth.

INTERESTING FACT: FRILLNECK LIZARDS CAN RUN EXTREMELY FAST, SOMETIMES ON TWO LEGS, WHEN ESCAPING DANGER.

FRILLNECK LIZARD

G IS FOR . . .

| SCIENTIFIC NAME: EOLOPHUS ROSEICAPILLA | SIZE: 30-36 CENTIMETRES TALL |

Galahs are one of the most widespread and well-loved parrots in Australia. They are also known as rose-breasted cockatoos.

Found all over the country, in both rural and urban areas, galahs often form large, noisy flocks to feed. They mostly eat seeds found on the ground and may travel long distances in search of good feeding grounds. In some farming areas, galahs are considered pests as their feeding behaviour can be damaging to crops.

Galahs build leaf-lined nests in tree hollows and form monogamous pairs. Galah parents share responsibility for incubating the eggs and caring for their young.

INTERESTING FACT: IN AUSTRALIAN SLANG, 'GALAH' IS USED TO DESCRIBE A SILLY OR FOOLISH PERSON.

GALAH

H IS FOR...

SCIENTIFIC NAME: THINORNIS CUCULLATUS	SIZE: 19-23 CENTIMETRES TALL

The hooded plover, also known as the hooded dotteral, is a small coastal bird found in various parts of southern Australia.

Hooded plovers live mostly on sandy beaches, where they can be seen in pairs or small groups hopping around the water's edge, looking for insects or soldier crabs to eat.

They are endangered, with a population of less than 7000 across Australia. The main threat to their survival is disturbance from humans, dogs and horses on the beaches and in the sandy dunes where they build their nests and breed.

INTERESTING FACT: HOODED PLOVERS OFTEN DECORATE THEIR NESTS BY ENCIRCLING THEM WITH PEBBLES, SEAWEED OR OTHER BEACH DEBRIS.

HOODED PLOVER

I IS FOR . . .

SCIENTIFIC NAME: DELIAS HARPALYCE | SIZE: 6.7-7.2 CENTIMETRE WINGSPAN

The beautiful imperial jezebel butterfly is one of 225 species of jezebels that live across Australia and Asia. The imperial jezebel is found in the eucalypt forests of Victoria and New South Wales.

The females have a wingspan of 72 millimetres, while the males' is slightly smaller at 67 millimetres. Their brightly coloured wings serve as a warning to scare off potential predators.

These butterflies lay their eggs on mistletoe plants and, when they hatch, the caterpillars grow to about 4 centimetres long before building their cocoons and turning into butterflies.

INTERESTING FACT: IMPERIAL JEZEBEL CATERPILLARS EAT THEIR OWN EGGSHELLS AFTER THEY ARE BORN.

IMPERIAL JEZEBEL

J IS FOR . . .

SCIENTIFIC NAME: EPHIPPIORHYNCHUS ASIATICUS | SIZE: 1.3–1.5 METRES TALL

Jabirus are the only native Australian stork and also the country's largest wetland bird. They are found in wetlands, mudlands and swamps across northern and eastern Australia.

Though commonly known as jabirus in Australia, they are officially called black-necked storks, a misleading name as their glossy, green and purple necks only appear black from a distance.

Jabirus form long-term pairs but usually forage and hunt alone, feeding on large insects, crustaceans, fish, eels and amphibians. They build nests in tall trees in or around the water and return to them year after year. Jabiru couples share responsibility for incubating the eggs and feeding their young.

INTERESTING FACT: THE NAME 'JABIRU' IS COMMONLY BELIEVED TO BE AN INDIGENOUS TERM, BUT IS IN FACT A BRAZILIAN NAME FOR A DIFFERENT SPECIES OF STORK.

JABIRU

K IS FOR . . .

SCIENTIFIC NAME: PHASCOLARCTOS CINEREUS | SIZE: 60-85 CENTIMETRES LONG

Koalas are one of Australia's most well-loved and recognised animals. They are often called 'koala bears', but they are not bears at all. Koalas are marsupials, which means they carry their babies in their pouch until they are well developed. They are not social animals, with the only real bond occurring between a mother and its dependent young.

A koala's diet consists entirely of eucalyptus leaves, but while there are more than 700 species of eucalypt in Australia, koalas will eat from less than 50 of these. Because eucalyptus leaves have a high moisture content, koalas rarely need to drink water.

Koalas are endangered and are most threatened by loss of suitable habitat. They are also very vulnerable to bushfires as they are slow moving and often unable to escape.

INTERESTING FACT: KOALAS SLEEP UP TO 20 HOURS A DAY.

KOALA

L IS FOR . . .

SCIENTIFIC NAME: CERCARTETUS LEPIDUS	SIZE: 5-6 CENTIMETRES LONG

The little pygmy possum, the world's smallest possum, is also known as the Tasmanian pygmy possum, as they were initially thought to exist only in Tasmania. However, small populations have also been found in South Australia, mostly on Kangaroo Island.

Little pygmy possums, which look more like mice than possums, are marsupials that spend the majority of their time in low branches of trees. They are nocturnal, solitary animals that only bond with their own young.

Little pygmy possums feed on insects, spiders, small lizards, nectar and pollen, mostly from banksia and eucalyptus trees.

INTERESTING FACT: LITTLE PYGMY POSSUMS HAVE STRONG TAILS THAT CAN SUPPORT THEIR ENTIRE BODY WEIGHT.

LITTLE
PYGMY POSSUM

M IS FOR . . .

| SCIENTIFIC NAME: PSEPHOTUS VARIUS | SIZE: 27-32 CENTIMETRES TALL |

The colourful mulga parrot is found throughout arid regions, scrublands and woodlands of interior and southern Australia. They are often found in mulga trees, hence their name, but they also nest in many other trees.

Like most parrots, mulga parrots form monogamous pairs. They eat seeds of grasses, flowers and fruit, usually feeding in pairs or small family groups. They are much quieter than other parrots and, unlike most of their relatives, they do not form large flocks.

Mulga parrots build their nests in tree hollows and line them with wood chips. The females are responsible for incubating the eggs but both parents help raise their chicks.

INTERESTING FACT: THE MULGA PARROT'S SCIENTIFIC NAME, 'PSEPHOTUS', MEANS 'INLAID WITH SMALL PEBBLES' AFTER ITS INTRICATE FEATHERED CHEEK PATTERNS.

MULGA PARROT

N IS FOR . . .

SCIENTIFIC NAME: MYRMECOBIUS FASCIATUS | SIZE: 35-45 CENTIMETRES LONG

The numbat, sometimes called the banded anteater,
is a small marsupial native to Western Australia.

Numbats are rarely seen, as their size and appearance
enable them to blend into their surroundings, and they
dart into cover, usually hollow logs, at any sign of danger.
They feed exclusively on termites, needing to eat up
to 20,000 a day.

Numbats are the only marsupials that are fully active
during the day, when they spend most of their time
looking for termites. They have the best vision of all
marsupials and, like most ant-eating species, have
very long tongues.

INTERESTING FACT: NUMBATS HAVE MORE TEETH THAN
ANY OTHER LAND MAMMAL, BUT THEY ARE UNDERDEVELOPED
AND NOT USED FOR EATING.

NUMBAT

O IS FOR . . .

SCIENTIFIC NAME: NEOPHEMA CHRYSOGASTER | SIZE: 20-22 CENTIMETRES TALL

The orange-bellied parrot is one of the rarest and most endangered species in Australia. They are primarily found in Tasmania where they breed exclusively during the summer months, before migrating to coastal regions of Victoria and South Australia for winter.

Orange-bellied parrots mate for life and nest high in the hollow eucalyptus trees adjacent to their coastal feeding grounds of buttongrass plains. They lay clutches of up to six eggs but usually no more than three chicks survive.

These beautiful parrots are critically endangered, with less than 50 remaining in the wild. Their habitat continues to disappear, and they also face competition from introduced birds like sparrows for food, as well as threats from feral cats and foxes.

INTERESTING FACT: ORANGE-BELLIED PARROTS TAKE A BREAK ON THEIR MIGRATION TO SNACK ON BEACH VEGETATION ON KING ISLAND.

ORANGE-BELLIED PARROT

P IS FOR . . .

SCIENTIFIC NAME: ORNITHORHYNCHUS ANATINUS | SIZE: 43-50 CENTIMETRES LONG

The platypus is one of the world's most unusual animals and is found in rivers and streams on the east coast of mainland Australia and in Tasmania. They are shy, solitary monotremes, which, along with echidnas, are the only mammals that lay eggs.

Platypuses use neither sight, sound nor smell to hunt. Instead, their primary sensory organ is their duck-like bill, which has electroreceptors that detect electrical currents caused by the movement of their prey, and pressure-sensitive receptors.

Platypuses are carnivores and mostly eat worms and crustaceans that they dig up in riverbeds with their bills. Both male and female platypuses have spurs on their back feet, but only the males' contain venom, which is thought to be used to assert dominance during the breeding season.

INTERESTING FACTS: PLATYPUSES DON'T HAVE A STOMACH AND THEIR TEETH DROP OUT AS BABIES AND NEVER GROW BACK.

PLATYPUS

Q IS FOR . . .

SCIENTIFIC NAME: SETONIX BRACHYURUS	SIZE: 40-50 CENTIMETRES TALL

One of the smallest species of wallaby, quokkas are only found in a few tiny areas of Western Australia - on the mainland and on Rottnest Island and Bald Island.

Quokkas seem to prefer areas that have been burned by bushfires in the previous ten years. They are browsing herbivores that eat a variety of plants but show particular preference for new young growth. Quokkas are also good tree climbers and often do so to reach food.

Quokkas are endangered, with mainland quokkas under considerably more pressure than those on the islands, due to the impact of introduced foxes and feral cats, as well as deforestation and destruction of habitat, caused primarily by feral pigs.

INTERESTING FACT: THE TREND OF TAKING SELFIES WITH THE UNAFRAID AND SEEMINGLY SMILING QUOKKA HAS LED TO THEM BEING CALLED THE HAPPIEST ANIMAL IN THE WORLD.

QUOKKA

R IS FOR . . .

SCIENTIFIC NAME: MACROPUS RUFUS	SIZE: UP TO 2 METRES TALL

The red kangaroo is the largest of all kangaroo species and Australia's largest native land mammal. Males are larger than females and weigh about 85 kilograms. Red kangaroos can live for up to 23 years.

They are extremely powerful jumpers, able to leap 2 metres high and more than 8 metres forward in a single bound. Red kangaroos can hop at speeds of over 60 kilometres per hour.

Red kangaroos live across most parts of Australia, except Tasmania. They live in small groups of around ten but are sometimes seen gathered in the hundreds or even thousands, especially near a reliable food source during times of drought.

INTERESTING FACT: RED KANGAROOS FIGHT ONE ANOTHER BY BOXING WITH THEIR PAWS, BUT IF A FIGHT ESCALATES, THEY CAN STAND ON THEIR TAILS AND KICK WITH BOTH LEGS.

RED KANGAROO

S IS FOR . . .

SCIENTIFIC NAME: PETAURUS BREVICEPS | SIZE: 16-20 CENTIMETRES LONG

The sugar glider is a small marsupial that lives in the trees of northern and eastern Australia.

Sugar gliders are unique in their ability to glide from tree to tree, both to avoid predators and to find food. A soft, furry membrane called a patagium on each side of their bodies allows them to glide.

Sugar gliders are social creatures that live in groups of several adults and their young in tree hollows. They are nocturnal, spending their days huddled together in their nests and their nights gliding through the trees eating sap, nectar, pollen and insects.

INTERESTING FACT: SUGAR GLIDERS CAN GLIDE UP TO 45 METRES IN ONE LEAP.

SUGAR GLIDER

T IS FOR...

SCIENTIFIC NAME: SARCOPHILUS HARRISII | SIZE: 55-65 CENTIMETRES LONG

Tasmanian devils are the world's largest carnivorous marsupial. Despite their small size, devils can appear very fierce with their unique, spine-chilling screech. This led to European settlers naming them devils.

Devils are limited to Tasmania now but it is believed they once roamed the mainland of Australia before the arrival of the dingo. They are nocturnal scavengers with powerful jaws that allow them to eat their prey completely – bones, fur and all. Famous for rowdy communal feeding habits, devils use various noises and displays to establish dominance within the pack.

Tasmanian devils are seriously endangered since the discovery of Devil Facial Tumour Disease in the 1990s. This fatal, infectious and so-far incurable disease has wiped out much of the population and scientists are working hard to find a cure before it's too late.

INTERESTING FACT: THE DEVIL'S FAMOUS GAPE STEMS MORE FROM FEAR AND UNCERTAINTY THAN FROM AGGRESSION.

TASMANIAN DEVIL

U IS FOR . . .

SCIENTIFIC NAME: PETROGALE INORNATA | SIZE: 49-59 CENTIMETRES TALL

The unadorned rock wallaby is a sub-species of rock wallaby. While they get their name from their plain, pale fur, their fur colour is quite variable within the species and tends to closely resemble the colour of rocks and soil in their habitat.

They live predominantly in coastal regions of North Queensland. Like all rock wallabies, unadorned rock wallabies prefer boulder fields and rocky outcrops in coastal scrublands and open forests.

Unadorned rock wallabies are marsupials, raising their young in pouches. They eat a range of foods, including grasses, shrubs, seeds and flowers. They live in both small and large groups, sometimes numbering over 100, and compete among one another for the best rocky shelters.

INTERESTING FACT: LIKE ALL WALLABIES, UNADORNED ROCK WALLABIES PRODUCE TWO TYPES OF MILK, ONE FOR BABIES AND ONE FOR OLDER OFFSPRING.

UNADORNED ROCK WALLABY

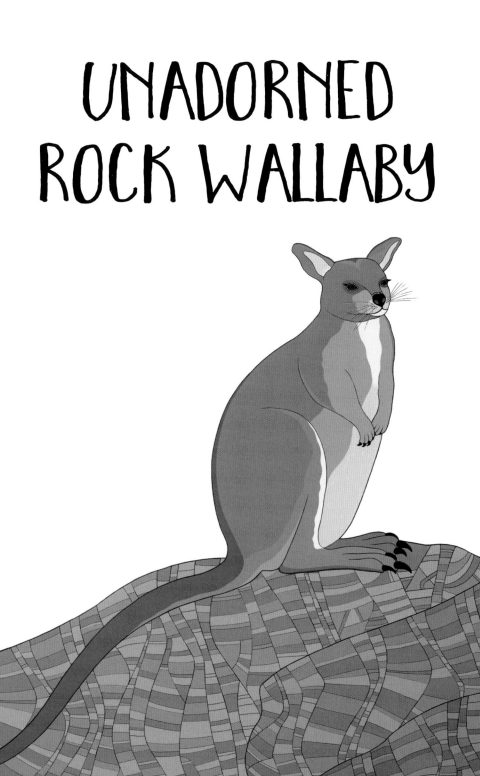

V IS FOR . . .

SCIENTIFIC NAME: MALURUS LAMBERTI	SIZE: 13-15 CENTIMETRES TALL

The variegated fairy-wren is the most widespread of the nine species of fairy-wren found in Australia.

These little wrens are renowned for their colours, but in fact it is only the males that display such bright feathers, and only in breeding season. Non-breeding males, females and juveniles are mostly brownish-grey in colour, although some sub-species have more blueish-grey feathers.

Variegated fairy-wrens live in a variety of habitats, from forests, woodlands and scrublands to suburban gardens and coastal regions. They feed mostly on insects and stay close to the shrubbery, rarely venturing out into the open.

Variegated fairy-wrens live in small groups consisting of a monogamous pair with several helper birds to help raise the young.

INTERESTING FACT: MALE WRENS PICK YELLOW PETALS AND DISPLAY THEM TO ATTRACT A FEMALE.

VARIEGATED FAIRY-WREN

W IS FOR . . .

SCIENTIFIC NAME: VOMBATUS URSINUS | SIZE: 0.8–1.2 METRES LONG

Wombats are one of Australia's most beloved animals. They are found throughout south-east Australia and Tasmania in all sorts of habitats, from coastal to alpine.

Wombats grow to around 1 metre in length and can weigh between 20 and 35 kilograms. They are mostly nocturnal, spending their nights grazing on various grasses, tubers and plant roots, but in winter they will sometimes come out during the day to bask in the sun.

Wombats are somewhat famous for their poo, which is cube-shaped and the driest of any mammal. This is thought to be because they have an incredibly long digestive process, lasting 14 to 18 days.

INTERESTING FACT: WOMBATS HAVE BACKWARD POUCHES TO PROTECT THEIR JOEYS FROM DIRT WHEN DIGGING BURROWS.

WOMBAT

X IS FOR . . .

COMMON NAME: MACLEAY'S HONEYEATER | SIZE: 17-21 CENTIMETRES TALL

The *Xanthotis macleayanus* is a species of honeyeater that is better known by its common name, Macleay's honeyeater.

They are endemic to the wet, tropical regions of Far North Queensland where they inhabit rainforests, mangroves, gardens and banana plantations.

These honeyeaters are harder to spot than most other species as they tend to live higher up in the rainforests. Their diet consists of about 70 per cent insects and spiders and 30 per cent nectar and fruit. This kind of diet means they play an important part in the pollination of rainforest plants.

INTERESTING FACT: THERE ARE 187 SPECIES OF HONEYEATER AND ABOUT HALF OF THESE ARE NATIVE TO AUSTRALIA.

XANTHOTIS MACLEAYANUS

y IS FOR . . .

SCIENTIFIC NAME: CALYPTORHYNCHUS FUNEREUS | SIZE: 55–65 CENTIMETRES TALL

The yellow-tailed black cockatoo is one of Australia's largest cockatoo species. They are found in south-eastern Australia, from South Australia to the southern and central regions of Queensland.

Their favourite habitats are eucalypt forests and pine plantations. Yellow-tailed black cockatoos build nests in tree hollows which they line with wood chips. The female incubates the eggs while the male brings her food.

In the past, yellow-tailed black cockatoos fed mostly on seeds of native trees, such as banksias and casuarinas, as well as wood-boring grubs, which they reach by tearing bark off tree trunks with their extremely strong beaks. With the more recent establishment of pine plantations, these noisy cockatoos are often seen pecking open pinecones to eat the seeds inside.

INTERESTING FACT: YELLOW-TAILED BLACK COCKATOO CHICKS ARE BORN WITH PINK BEAKS THAT TURN GREY AFTER ABOUT THREE MONTHS.

YELLOW-TAILED BLACK COCKATOO

Z IS FOR . . .

SCIENTIFIC NAME: TAENIOPYGIA GUTTATA	SIZE: 10–11 CENTIMETRES TALL

The zebra finch is the most common and widespread of Australia's native finch species, being found across much of mainland Australia. They are social birds that live in large flocks of 100 or more.

Zebra finches feed on the ground, mainly on grass seeds which they de-husk with their short, strong beaks. They also eat insects, especially when they are feeding their young.

Zebra finches mate for life and often breed after heavy rainfall, when there is plenty of food available for their young. The male gathers materials for their nests, which the female then constructs. Both parents share responsibility for looking after their young.

INTERESTING FACT: ZEBRA FINCHES CAN BREED FROM AROUND 75 DAYS OLD, MAKING THEM THE WORLD'S FASTEST-MATURING BIRD.

ZEBRA FINCH

ACKNOWLEDGEMENTS

I am incredibly lucky to be surrounded by so many great people who all help bring books like this to life.

First, to the wonderfully supportive team at Lothian who publish my books, especially Kate Stevens, my publisher, whose support and belief in me has actually changed my world – thank you!

As always, a big thanks to my mum, Gail, and my sister, Jo-Maree, for their help with research and proofreading. Without you I'd still be wondering about the relevance of tectonic plates!

My team at Red Parka – you are amazing! A few years ago Red Parka was just me drawing little pictures in my bedroom, and now, it's all of us creating art and joy together every day! Katie, Rebecca, Greta, Rachel, Rhi, Amelia, Emma, Ethan and Charles . . . I love you like family. Thank you for being part of my crazy dream and bringing so much more to Red Parka than I could ever create alone.

Last, and most of all, thanks to my beautiful family – Tracy and Tess. I love you all the books in the world!

ABOUT THE AUTHOR

Jennifer Cossins is an award-winning Tasmanian artist and writer with a passion for nature, the animal kingdom and all things bright and colourful.

A born and bred Tasmanian, Jennifer also designs textiles, homewares and stationery, which she stocks in her store, Red Parka, in Hobart, Tasmania.

Jennifer's other books include *The Baby Animal Book*, *101 Collective Nouns* and the CBCA Honour Book *A-Z of Endangered Animals*.

REDPARKA.COM.AU

THE END